Patterson Elementary School
3731 Lawrence Drive
Naperville, IL. 60564

EVERYDAY SCIENCE

Floating
and Sinking

Please visit our web site at: www.garethstevens.com
For a free color catalog describing Gareth Stevens Publishing's list of high-quality books
and multimedia programs, call 1-800-542-2595 or fax your request to (414) 332-3567.

Library of Congress Cataloging-In-Publication Data

Riley, Peter D.
    Floating and sinking / by Peter Riley. — North American ed.
        p. cm. — (Everyday science)
    Summary: Explores why some objects float in water and others sink, providing
ideas for simple demonstrations of related concepts.
    Includes bibliographical references and index.
    Contents: Float — Or sink — Sorting materials — Which floats? — Water pushes
up — Watch the water — Hollow or solid? — Fill it up — Boats — Make it float — Boat
loads — Which sinks?
    ISBN 0-8368-3248-5 (lib. bdg.)
    1. Floating bodies—Juvenile literature. [1. Floating bodies.] I. Title.
QC147.5.R54   2002
532'.25—dc21   2002022634

This North American edition first published in 2002 by
Gareth Stevens Publishing
A World Almanac Education Group Company
330 West Olive Street, Suite 100
Milwaukee, Wisconsin 53212 USA

Original text © 2001 by Peter Riley. Images © 2001 by Franklin Watts.
First published in 2001 by Franklin Watts, 96 Leonard Street, London, EC2A 4XD, England.
This U.S. edition © 2002 by Gareth Stevens, Inc.

Series Editor: Rachel Cooke
Designers: Jason Anscomb, Michael Leamen Design Partnership
Photography: Ray Moller (unless otherwise credited)
Gareth Stevens Editor: Lizz Baldwin

Picture Credits: Images Colour Library, p. 7 (t); Oxford Scientific Films/Deni Bowm, p. 6 (t); Pictor International, p. 12;
The Stock Market/Lester Lefkowitz, p. 6 (b).

The original publisher thanks the following children for modeling for this book: Jordan Conn, Nicola Freeman, Charley Gibbens,
Alex Jordan, Eddie Lengthorn, and Rachael Moodley.

Printed in Hong Kong

1 2 3 4 5 6 7 8 9 06 05 04 03 02

Floating
and Sinking

Written by Peter Riley

Gareth Stevens Publishing
A WORLD ALMANAC EDUCATION GROUP COMPANY

About This Book

Everyday Science is designed to encourage children to think about their everyday world in a scientific way, by examining cause and effect through close observation and discussing what they have seen. Here are some tips to help you get the most from **Floating and Sinking**.

- This book introduces the basic concepts of floating and sinking and some of the vocabulary associated with them, such as water level, load, and the comparison of hollow and solid, and it prepares children for more advanced learning about floating and sinking.

- On pages 9, 13, 19, and 25, children are asked to predict the results of a particular action or activity. Be sure to discuss the reasons for any answers they give before turning the page. Most of these activities have only one possible result. Discuss the reasons for each result, then set up other activities for the children and discuss possible outcomes.

- This book offers many opportunities to discuss force and movement. On pages 12 and 13, for example, children can explore the concept of weight as a downward force, and on page 11, they can learn that objects of the same size do not necessarily weigh the same.

- Even if you do not carry out the tests suggested in the book, you can use them to teach children how to conduct experiments. If, for example, the containers on page 24 were different sizes, would this experiment still be a fair test?

- When using the word "solid," you may need to explore its other meaning, a state of matter, that is, a solid as compared to a liquid or a gas. Discuss both meanings of the word and the relationship of the two meanings.

Contents

Float

Some things float.
Some things sink.

Leaves float
on a stream.

Ships float
on the sea.

Or **Sink**

Pebbles sink in a pond.

Soap sinks in
a bowl of water.

Sorting **Materials**

Lucy has some objects that are each made of a different material.

plastic fork

cork

sponge

coin

marble

wood block

metal spoon

She wants to see which materials will float
and which will sink if she puts them in water.

Lucy made a chart of her predictions.

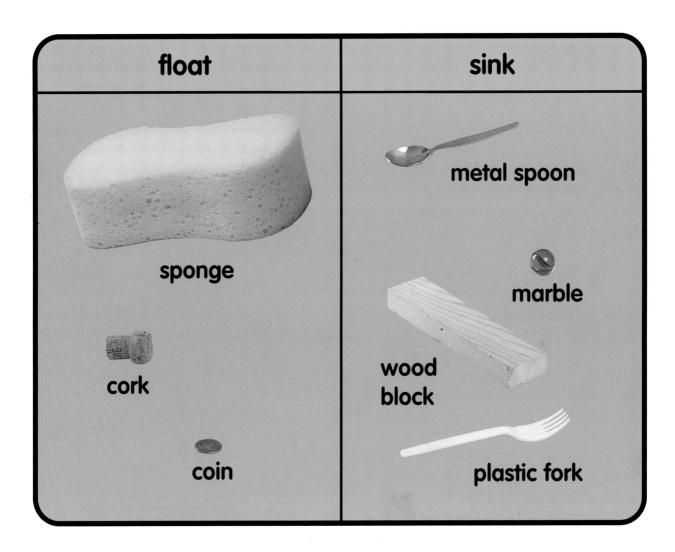

float	sink
sponge	metal spoon
cork	marble
coin	wood block
	plastic fork

Write down your predictions, too.
What do you think will happen?
Turn the page to find out.

Which 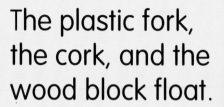 Floats?

The plastic fork, the cork, and the wood block float.

The marble, the coin, and the metal spoon sink.

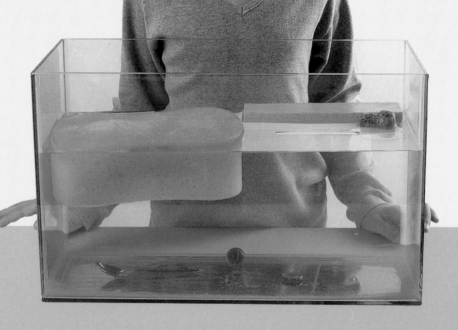

The sponge filled with water but floated just below the surface. Were Lucy's predictions right? Were your predictions right?

Carl has a brick and a piece of wood that are about the same size. He wants to see if they will float.

The wood is light in weight. It floats in water.

The brick is heavy. It sinks in water.

Water  Pushes Up

Water pushes up on objects.

The push of water is strong enough to make
lightweight materials, such as wood, float.
Even large logs float.

Feel the push of water yourself.

Screw the lid tightly onto an empty plastic bottle.

Push the bottle underwater, then take your hand away.

What happens? Turn the page to find out.

Watch the Water

The bottle rises through the water and floats on the surface.

The strong push of the water makes the bottle move quickly.

Pour some water into a clear bowl.

Put a mark on the bowl at the top of the water level.

Slowly push an empty bottle, with a lid on it, into the water. The water level goes up.

What do you think will happen when you take the bottle out of the water?

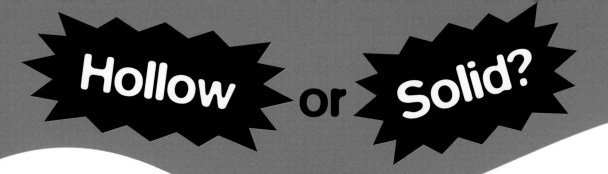

Some objects are hollow. They have air inside them.

An empty bottle is hollow. It is full of air.

Hollow objects float because the air inside them makes them lightweight.

Some objects are solid.
They have no air inside them.

piece
of wood

rock

Solid objects made of heavy materials sink.
Solid objects made of lightweight materials float.

Fill It Up

Adam fills an empty bottle with sand.

He puts the bottle into water.

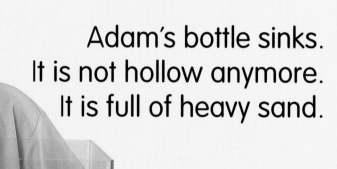

Adam's bottle sinks.
It is not hollow anymore.
It is full of heavy sand.

Natasha puts a marble into an empty bottle.

She puts the bottle into water.

Will the bottle float or sink? Turn the page to find out.

19

Boats

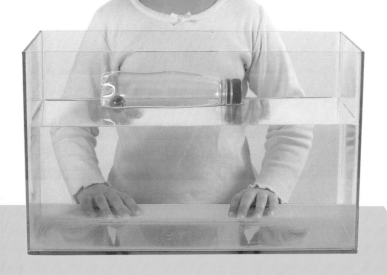

Natasha's bottle floats. The bottle is still hollow. It still has lots of air in it.

A boat is hollow.
It has air between its sides.

When you put a small load into the boat, you push out some of the air.

The weight of the load makes the boat sink a little in the water.

If you put a very large load into the boat, you push out most of the air.

The weight of this load is too heavy for the water to push up, so the boat sinks.

Make It Float

Make a ball of
polymer clay.

Put the ball
into water.

The ball is solid, not
hollow, so it sinks.

Make a dish out
of polymer clay.

Put the dish into water.

The dish is
hollow, so
it floats.

How small can you make the sides of the
dish and still keep it floating?

Boat Loads

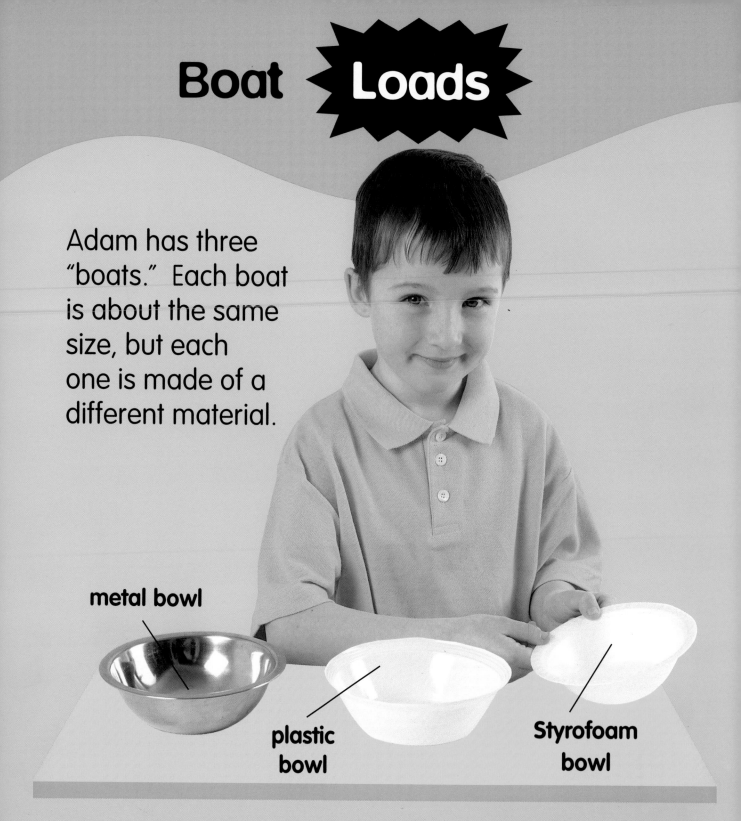

Adam has three "boats." Each boat is about the same size, but each one is made of a different material.

metal bowl

plastic bowl

Styrofoam bowl

Adam tests the boats and finds out that they all float.

Then he sees which boat can hold the biggest load.

He adds marbles to each boat until the boat sinks.

Which boat do you think will hold the fewest marbles? Turn the page to find out.

Which

The metal "boat" is the first to sink.

Adam made a chart of his results.

	metal bowl	plastic bowl	Styrofoam bowl
first	✔		
second		✔	
third			✔

Try Adam's test and make a chart of your results. Are your results the same as Adam's?

Make boats of different shapes using the same
amount of polymer clay for each one.
Try Adam's test with your clay boats.

Which shape holds the most
marbles before the boat sinks?

Useful Words

experiment: a test that is done to find out whether or not an idea is correct.

float: to stay on or near the surface of water and not sink.

hollow: having empty space inside.

load: the weight of objects being carried.

material: a type of solid matter, such as wood, metal, or plastic, that is used to make objects.

polymer clay: a plastic modeling compound, such as Fimo or Sculpy.

prediction: a guess made before a test. The test proves if the prediction was right or wrong.

sink: to fall slowly in water, below the surface, and not float.

solid: not having any space inside.

surface: the outside of something. The surface of water is where the water meets the air.

water level: the height water reaches in a container.

weight: the measure of how heavy an object is.

Some Answers

Here are some answers to the questions asked in this book. If you had different answers, you may be right, too. Talk over your answers with other people and see if you can explain why they are right.

page 10   Lucy's predictions were right except for the coin, which sinks, and the wood block and plastic fork, both of which float. Your predictions may have been different from Lucy's, so you may have different results. Try the test yourself using objects made of other materials.

page 15   When you take the bottle out, the water level goes down to where it was before you put the bottle into the water.

page 23   The only way you can find out the answer to this question is by testing a dish yourself. Make the polymer clay as thin as possible to help the dish float better. Also, be sure there are no holes in the bottom of the dish.

page 27   The only way to answer this question is to do the test. Make sure the test is fair by using the same amount of polymer clay for each boat. Make a round boat, a square boat, and an oval boat. Think about the different shapes of boats you see in real life. Before you start the test, guess which boat will hold the most marbles. Be sure to make a record of your test results to see if your guesses were right.

For More Information

More Books to Read

- *Let's Try It Out in the Water.*
Seymour Simon and Nicole Fauteux
(Simon & Schuster)

- *The Magic School Bus Ups and Downs: A Book
About Floating and Sinking*
Joanna Cole, Bruce Degen, and Jane B. Mason
(Econo-Clad Books)

- *Tell Me How Ships Float. Whiz Kids* (series)
Shirley Willis
(Franklin Watts)

Web Sites

- BrainPOP: Buoyancy
www.brainpop.com/science/forces/buoyancy

- Nova Online: Buoyancy Basics
www.pbs.org/wgbh/nova/lasalle/buoybasics.html

Index